Me

in the Eucharist

Fr Stephen Wang

*All booklets are published
thanks to the generosity of the supporters
of the Catholic Truth Society*

All rights reserved. First published 2018 by The Incorporated Catholic Truth Society, 40-46 Harleyford Road London SE11 5AY Tel: 020 7640 0042 Fax: 020 7640 0040.

Text copyright © Fr Stephen Wang, 2018. Images by Elizabeth Wang, copyright © Radiant Light 2000, www.radiantlight.org.uk

ISBN 978 1 78469 566 8

Acknowledgements

Note about the artist

The paintings reproduced in this booklet are by Elizabeth Wang. Elizabeth was born in 1942, received into the Catholic Church in 1968, and died in 2016. She was an artist, housewife and mother who spent much of her time writing and speaking about prayer and the Catholic faith. She was very involved in the life of her home parish of Our Lady of Lourdes, Harpenden.

Over five thousand of her paintings can be seen online, together with many of her writings, at the Radiant Light website. Please visit: *www.radiantlight.org.uk*

Quotations from the saints are, as far as the publisher is aware, in the public domain. If any are not and need an appropriate copyright acknowledgement, please advise the publisher, and these will be corrected in any future reprints.

Much of the material in this booklet was first published by the Agency for Evangelisation of the Diocese of Westminster in their Lent 2018 booklet *"We Adore You, O Christ, and We Praise You": The Gift of the Holy Eucharist*. It is reprinted here with permission. The publishers would like to acknowledge their thanks to the Diocese of Westminster.

Contents

Introduction

This booklet was written to help people grow in their love for Christ in the Holy Eucharist, and to help parish communities deepen their Eucharistic faith. This is Pope Francis's wish for the whole Church: "Without prolonged moments of adoration, of prayerful encounter with the word, of sincere conversation with the Lord, our work easily becomes meaningless... I want to encourage everyone to visit...the Blessed Sacrament of the infinite love of Christ and his mercy."

It is a sentiment echoed in our own country by Cardinal Vincent Nichols who has written: "We seek to rejuvenate Eucharistic adoration in our parishes as the source of strength for our lives and for our mission, that of making present the love and compassion of Jesus in our society".

The booklet does not cover every aspect of the Mass, and many important things are left out. Instead, the chapters focus on the sacramental presence of Jesus Christ, especially his Real Presence in the Blessed Sacrament and its implications for our lives.

There are six main themes: the Christian encounter with the Lord ("I Will Be with You Always"); the Real Presence of Christ in the Eucharist; the Holy Sacrifice of the Mass;

Illustration on facing page: *"If we draw close to Christ, the Light of the World, we share in his holiness, and we are sheltered by his glory"* (Image Code: T-01269-OL)

the graces given in Holy Communion ("Sacred Banquet, Spiritual Food"); Adoration of the Blessed Sacrament; and the implications of the Mass for service and mission ("Love One Another as I Have Loved You").

The materials here are mainly for personal reading and reflection, but they can easily be used in group discussions and faith sharing groups. These could be run in parishes during Lent or Advent or at any other time in the liturgical year. See the chapter "How to Run a Faith Sharing Group" at the end of this booklet for advice about how to run such a group.

The images reproduced here are by Catholic artist Elizabeth Wang, and they form a core part of the materials, allowing for personal meditation and group reflection on the mystery of Eucharist. The final prayers for each session are taken from the Rite of Eucharistic Adoration and Benediction. "*CCC*" stands for the *Catechism of the Catholic Church*.

"I Will Be with You Always": The Christian Encounter with the Lord

Reflection

Many of us have a sincere faith, but we wish it were more alive and more life-giving. Sometimes we are not very aware of God's presence in our lives, and we wonder if Jesus has disappeared or forgotten us. Faith can feel very empty. The doubts can creep in very easily.

It's so important to remember the solemn promise he made to us after his Resurrection: "Behold, I am with you always, even to the end of time." Jesus Christ is Emmanuel: "God with us." He is the eternal Word who came to dwell among us. And even after his Ascension into heaven, he is present with us now, through the gift of the Holy Spirit, and through the life of the Church. He has not left us alone. We just need eyes to see and ears to hear.

There are many different ways that Jesus speaks to us and touches our lives. It's often in very personal ways: through an event, an encounter, a conversation; through an experience of beauty, or kindness, or even of suffering; through the voice of conscience or the needs of those around us; through a moment of prayer, or a line from the

Illustration on facing page: *"Christ is present in our lives and in the Church, walking amongst his people"* (Image Code: T-01327-OL)

Holy Scriptures, or an unexpected inspiration from the Holy Spirit.

Jesus made a special promise to be with us through the liturgy and the sacraments. In each of the seven sacraments the great gift of salvation is made present. Through these sacred signs we worship God, and his work of making us holy is carried out. This is especially true of the sacrament of the Holy Eucharist, the Mass, which is "the source and summit of the Christian life".

As Catholics, we try to go to Mass each Sunday, but it can become just a routine, and we often forget the staggering truth and beauty of what is happening. Whenever we go to Mass, the Lord is present in the praying community; he speaks to us through his Holy Word; we are united with Jesus in the sacrifice he offered on the cross for our salvation; we meet him, if we are able, in Holy Communion; we receive the power of his Holy Spirit; and we are united with the whole Church across time and space. It is the holiest act of worship possible on earth. We should be awestruck and amazed.

Sometimes we do feel inspired, sometimes we feel a bit dry; sometimes we feel very peaceful, sometimes we are completely distracted. What matters is that we are there, and that we are trying to be open to the Lord.

Faith is a gift, but it's also something we need to work at. We don't come to Mass as strangers or indifferent spectators. We want to be conscious of what we are doing and what is taking place. We want our hearts and minds to be open and attentive, so we can enter into the prayers and the worship.

This isn't always easy, especially if we are tired, or sick, or caring for young children. And God loves us and delights in the simple fact that we are there. But the more we can "pray the Mass" and enter into it in a personal way, the more it will touch us and transform us. The sacramental reality can bear fruit in our lives, and our Sunday worship will become truly life-giving and give us joy and strength for the week ahead.

Holy Scripture

For personal prayer, reflection and meditation

[Speaking to his disciples after his Resurrection] "And Jesus came and said to them, 'All authority in heaven and on earth has been given to me. Go therefore and make disciples of all nations, baptising them in the name of the Father and of the Son and of the Holy Spirit, and teaching them to obey everything that I have commanded you. And remember, I am with you always, to the end of the age.'" (*Mt* 28:18-20)

[Jesus said] "'Again, truly I tell you, if two of you agree on earth about anything you ask, it will be done for you by my Father in heaven. For where two or three are gathered in my name, I am there among them.'" (*Mt* 18:19-20)

[On the road to Emmaus] "When he was at the table with them, he took bread, blessed and broke it, and gave it to

them. Then their eyes were opened, and they recognised him; and he vanished from their sight. They said to each other, 'Were not our hearts burning within us while he was talking to us on the road, while he was opening the Scriptures to us?'" (*Lk* 24:30-32)

[From the Book of Revelation] "'See, the home of God is among mortals. He will dwell with them; they will be his people, and God himself will be with them; he will wipe every tear from their eyes. Death will be no more; mourning and crying and pain will be no more, for the first things have passed away.' And the one who was seated on the throne said, 'See, I am making all things new.'" (*Rv* 21:3-5)

Catholic teaching

*Key passages from the Catechism
and other Church documents*

Catechism of the Catholic Church (*CCC*) 1324: "The Eucharist is 'the source and summit of the Christian life.' [*LG* 11]"

Sacramentum Caritatis 2: "In the sacrament of the altar, the Lord meets us, men and women created in God's image and likeness (cf. *Gn* 1:27), and becomes our companion along the way."

CCC 1373: "'Christ Jesus, who died, yes, who was raised from the dead, who is at the right hand of God, who indeed intercedes for us,' is present in many ways to his Church: [*Rm* 8:34; cf. *LG* 48] in his word, in his Church's prayer, 'where two or three are gathered in my name,' [*Mt* 18:20] in the poor, the sick, and the imprisoned, [cf. *Mt* 25:31-46] in the sacraments of which he is the author, in the Sacrifice of the Mass, and in the person of the minister. But 'he is present...most especially in the Eucharistic species.' [*SC* 7]"

CCC 1325: "'The Eucharist is the efficacious sign and sublime cause of that communion in the divine life and that unity of the People of God by which the Church is kept in being. It is the culmination both of God's action sanctifying the world in Christ and of the worship men offer to Christ and through him to the Father in the Holy Spirit.' [Congregation of Rites, Instruction, *Eucharisticum Mysterium*, 6]"

Wisdom from the saints

"If we really understood the Mass, we would die of joy." St John Vianney

"We must not separate our life from the Eucharist. The moment we do so, something shatters." St Teresa of Calcutta

"Hear Mass daily; it will prosper the whole day. All your duties will be performed the better for it, and your soul will be stronger to bear its daily cross. The Mass is the most holy act of religion. It is the favourite devotion of the saints." St Peter Julian Eymard

Illustration on facing page: *"Jesus Christ is the Bridge to Heaven. His love on the cross saves us and his loving presence sustains us"* (Image Code: T-00081-OL)

"It is easier for the earth to exist without the sun than without the Holy Sacrifice of the Mass!" St Pio of Pietrelcina

"The Church and the world have a great need for Eucharistic worship. Jesus awaits us in this sacrament of love. Let us not refuse the time to go to meet him in adoration." Pope St John Paul II

Summary of core beliefs

- Jesus Christ promised to be present in our lives and in the Church for all time.

- Christ is present at Mass in different ways: in the praying community; through his Word; through the ministry of the priest; and above all in the Blessed Sacrament.

- The Eucharist is the source and summit of the Christian life.

Practical suggestions

- Renew your commitment to attend Mass each Sunday and Holy Day.

- Reflect on the Sunday Scripture readings sometime during the week before.

- Arrive a few minutes early for Mass so you have some time to pray and spiritually prepare.

- Keep Sunday special – by giving time for rest and prayer and family, and avoiding unnecessary work or shopping.

- Learn about the Mass – e.g. by reading the *Catechism of the Catholic Church*, the *YouCat* (the Youth Catechism of the Catholic Church), Catholic pamphlets, or online resources.

- Pray for your priest – that he can celebrate the Mass prayerfully and reverently, and that his preaching will be helpful.

Prayer

Lord,
may this sacrament of new life
warm our hearts with your love
and make us eager for the eternal joy of your kingdom.
We ask this through Christ our Lord.
R. Amen.

The Real Presence of Christ in the Eucharist

Reflection

Jesus Christ is present at the Mass in different ways: in the midst of the Christian community, when they gather to pray in his name; through his Word, when the Scriptures are proclaimed; and in the ministry of his priests, who act "in the person of Christ the head". There is one way of being present, however, that is utterly unique and has a significance far beyond all the others: the Real Presence of Jesus Christ in the Eucharist.

We believe that Jesus Christ, true God and true man, is present in Holy Communion, under the appearances of bread and wine, in what is called the Blessed Sacrament. At every Mass, at the consecration, the bread and wine are changed into the Body and Blood of Christ through the power of the Holy Spirit. This is the miracle of transubstantiation. It's why we teach children not to say "the bread" or "the wine" when speaking about Holy Communion, because something fundamental has changed.

This is not just a sign or a symbol or a memory. We encounter "the whole Christ" – Body, Blood, Soul and Divinity – heart to heart, face to face. He is here.

Illustration on facing page: *"Through the power of the Holy Spirit, and the ministry and words of the priest, Jesus Christ becomes present on our altars at Mass"* (Image Code: T-00157A-OL)

We believe that the Eucharist is food for our hungry souls; it is healing and forgiveness; it is love and friendship; it is a share in his holiness and a promise of eternal life; it is a communion with the Church which is his body; it is a union with our brothers and sisters spread throughout the world and throughout time.

We don't always *feel* this or *see* it with our bodily eyes; but we can *believe* it, and see it with the eyes of faith. We believe this because of the words and the promises of Jesus. He himself said: "This is my body…this is my blood…"; "Anyone who eats my flesh and drinks my blood has eternal life"; "My flesh is real food and my blood is real drink." We believe this because of the constant teaching of the Church over twenty centuries. And we believe this because of the witness of the saints, who became saints in part because they learned to love Jesus Christ in the Eucharist.

When St Claire of Assisi heard that Imperial troops were about to storm her city, she took the Blessed Sacrament to the window of her convent and prayed over the attacking armies. At the last minute, the power of her prayer and the power of the Sacrament miraculously turned them away. When St Margaret Mary Alacoque went to pray in front of the Blessed Sacrament in her convent in France, she had a vision of Jesus standing before her. His Sacred Heart was burning with love for her and for the whole of humanity, wounded by our sins and our lack of love, calling us to know him more, calling us to love him in the Blessed Sacrament.

Most of us, however, don't see him in this way. We need faith. As Jesus said to St Thomas after the Resurrection: "Blessed are those who have not seen and yet believe." And many people have an instinctive feeling for the holiness of our Catholic churches. They are sacred spaces because of the presence of the Blessed Sacrament in the tabernacle. People understand that something happens at the moment of consecration. They instinctively want to worship Christ, now present here at the altar, when the priest holds up the host and the chalice for adoration. They know that they can open their hearts to him in a very personal way, in repentance, trust, love and friendship, because of his loving presence.

Holy Scripture

For personal prayer, reflection and meditation

[On the road to Emmaus] "When Jesus was at the table with them, he took bread, blessed and broke it, and gave it to them. Then their eyes were opened, and they recognised him; and he vanished from their sight. They said to each other, 'Were not our hearts burning within us while he was talking to us on the road, while he was opening the Scriptures to us?'" (*Lk* 24:30-32)

[St Paul writes] "The cup of blessing that we bless, is it not a sharing in the blood of Christ? The bread that we break, is it not a sharing in the body of Christ? Because there is one bread, we who are many are one body, for we all partake of the one bread." (*1 Co* 10:16-17)

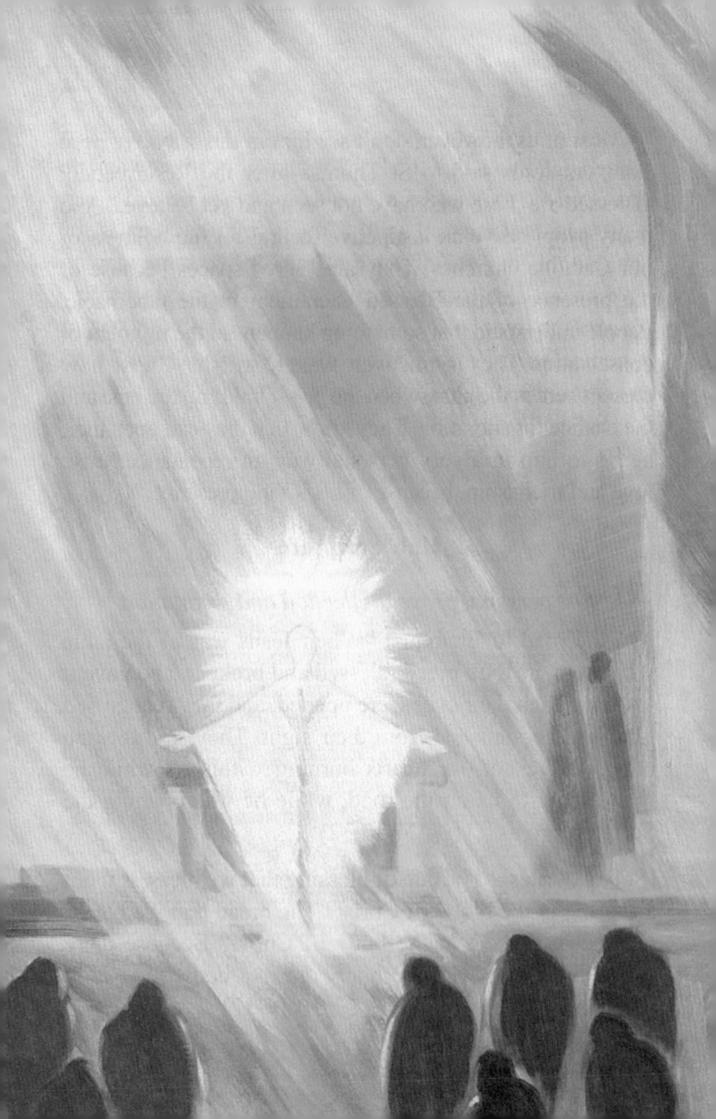

[St Paul writes] "For I received from the Lord what I also handed on to you, that the Lord Jesus on the night when he was betrayed took a loaf of bread, and when he had given thanks, he broke it and said, 'This is my body that is for you. Do this in remembrance of me.' In the same way he took the cup also, after supper, saying, 'This cup is the new covenant in my blood. Do this, as often as you drink it, in remembrance of me.' For as often as you eat this bread and drink the cup, you proclaim the Lord's death until he comes." (*1 Co* 11:23-26)

Catholic teaching

*Key passages from the Catechism
and other Church documents*

CCC 1374: "The mode of Christ's presence under the Eucharistic species is unique. It raises the Eucharist above all the sacraments as 'the perfection of the spiritual life and the end to which all the sacraments tend.' [St Thomas Aquinas, *STh* III, 73, 3c] In the most Blessed Sacrament of the Eucharist 'the Body and Blood, together with the Soul and Divinity, of our Lord Jesus Christ and, therefore, the whole Christ is truly, really, and substantially contained.' [Council of Trent (1551): *DS* 1651]"

CCC 1376: "The Council of Trent summarises the Catholic faith by declaring: '… by the consecration of the bread and wine there takes place a change of the whole substance of the bread into the substance of the Body of Christ our Lord

Illustration on facing page: *"Jesus Christ, our loving Saviour, is truly present with us after the consecration, in all his glory and majesty"* (Image Code: T-00375-OL)

and of the whole substance of the wine into the substance of his Blood. This change the holy Catholic Church has fittingly and properly called transubstantiation.' [Council of Trent (1551): *DS* 1642; cf. *Mt* 26:26 ff.; *Mk* 14:22 ff.; *Lk* 22:19 ff.; *1 Co* 11:24 ff.]"

CCC 1378: "'The Catholic Church has always offered and still offers to the sacrament of the Eucharist the cult of adoration, not only during Mass, but also outside of it, reserving the consecrated hosts with the utmost care, exposing them to the solemn veneration of the faithful, and carrying them in procession.' [Paul VI, *MF* 56]"

Presbyterorum Ordinis 5: "The Most Holy Eucharist contains the whole spiritual treasure of the Church, namely Christ himself, our Passover and our Living Bread".

Wisdom from the saints

"You left us yourself in the Sacrament of the Altar, and you opened wide your mercy to us. There is no misery that could exhaust you. You have called us all to this fountain of love, to this spring of God's compassion." St Faustina

"If I can give you any advice, I beg you to get closer to the Eucharist and to Jesus... We must pray to Jesus to give us that tenderness of the Eucharist." St Teresa of Calcutta

"Lord Jesus Christ, pierce my soul with your love so that I may always long for you alone, who are the bread of angels and the fulfilment of the soul's deepest desires. May my

Illustration on facing page: *"When Holy Communion is brought to the sick or housebound, Jesus Christ himself is present in the sacrament, sharing his light and his love"* (Image Code: T-01038B-OL)

heart always hunger for you, so that my soul may be filled with the sweetness of your presence." St Bonaventure

"We adore you, most holy Lord Jesus Christ, here, and in all your churches throughout all the world; and we bless you, because, by your holy cross, you have redeemed the world." St Francis of Assisi

"Many people nowadays say, 'I wish I could see his shape, his appearance, his clothes, his sandals.' Only look! You see him! You touch him! You eat him!" St John Chrysostom

Summary of core beliefs

- Jesus Christ is truly present in the Blessed Sacrament: the whole Christ – Body, Blood, Soul and Divinity.

- The bread and wine at Mass are changed into his Body and Blood through the miracle of transubstantiation, so that only the appearances and not the substance of bread and wine remain.

- We can worship Christ as God and Saviour in the Blessed Sacrament, and we can speak to him, heart to heart, as a friend and brother.

Practical suggestions

- Remember to genuflect as you enter and leave your place at Mass, and be conscious that you are genuflecting to the presence of Christ in the tabernacle.

- If you are able, you can kneel in prayer and adoration before Mass (to worship Christ and prepare for the celebration) and after Mass in thanksgiving.

- Appreciate the many gestures we make during Mass and what they signify: standing, kneeling, sitting; bowing during the Creed and as we approach Holy Communion, etc.

- As far as possible, try to keep a reverent and prayerful silence in church, and avoid unnecessary chatter – in order to help you be more prayerful, and to help those around you to pray.

- Display an image of the Sacred Heart of Jesus in your home, to remind you of his loving presence wherever you are.

Prayer

Lord our God,
in this great sacrament
we come into the presence of Jesus Christ, your Son,
born of the Virgin Mary
and crucified for our salvation.
May we who declare our faith
in this fountain of love and mercy
drink from it the water of everlasting life.
We ask this through Christ our Lord.
R. Amen.

The Holy Sacrifice of the Mass

Reflection

When Pope Benedict began his pontificate, he adopted the tradition of putting a fairly large crucifix in the centre of the altar when celebrating Mass. This annoyed a lot of people because it blocked their view of the Pope. They had come all this way to Rome and they couldn't see him. And this was the very point of doing it! Not to annoy people, but to remind them that the love of Jesus Christ on the cross is the centre of our Christian faith, and the centre of the Mass. We need to keep our focus constantly on him.

Catholic tradition speaks about "the Holy Sacrifice of the Mass." The Eucharist is more than a community meeting, more than a Liturgy of the Word, more than a communion service. It is also a sacrifice.

But if Jesus died on the cross, and "by a single offering has perfected for all time those who are sanctified" (*Heb* 10:14), how can there be another sacrifice? Does it mean his death on the cross was insufficient? Are we still waiting for our salvation to be accomplished?

The Church teaches that the Mass is a true and proper sacrifice, not because it is independent of the cross, but

because it re-presents the very sacrifice that Christ offered on the cross, and applies its power. We hear the language of sacrifice in the words of consecration that Jesus spoke at the Last Supper. He said, "This is my body *which is given for you*", and "This cup *that is poured out for you* is the new covenant in my blood." The sacrifice of Christ and the sacrifice of the Eucharist are one single sacrifice.

Jesus cannot die again, but we can be brought sacramentally into the presence of his saving death on the cross. We are united with the offering of Jesus on the cross and therefore with his eternal offering. The Eucharist is a memorial in the most profound sense because it makes a past event present for us today, and allows its effects to touch us today. This has so many implications.

It means we are brought close to the merciful love of Christ on the cross. We could not be there two thousand years ago but we can be there through the Mass. This should fill us with awe and wonder. The Mass is the holiest place on earth. There is no distance between us and our loving Saviour.

It means that even though salvation has been won for us, once and for all, on the cross, the *effects* of this salvation – the benefits, the graces, the fruits – are shared with us today through the Mass. The new covenant is renewed in an "un-bloody manner". The sacrifice of the Eucharist is an *effective* sacrifice, it allows our redemption to be accomplished, and brings graces for the living and the dead. It is a "sacrifice of propitiation" because it brings forgiveness for our daily sins.

It means that we can offer our lives, with Christ, to the Father through the Holy Spirit. My life can become part of his offering on the cross, and in this way my life can become a life-giving sacrifice of love.

Holy Scripture

For personal prayer, reflection and meditation

[At the Last Supper] "Then Jesus took a loaf of bread, and when he had given thanks, he broke it and gave it to them, saying, 'This is my body, which is given for you. Do this in remembrance of me.' And he did the same with the cup after supper, saying, 'This cup that is poured out for you is the new covenant in my blood.'" (*Lk* 22:19-20)

[From the Letter to the Hebrews] "But he holds his priesthood permanently, because he continues for ever. Consequently he is able for all time to save those who approach God through him, since he always lives to make intercession for them." (*Heb* 7:24-25)

[From the Letter to the Hebrews] "For by a single offering he has perfected for all time those who are sanctified." (*Heb* 10:14)

[St Peter writes] "Come to him, a living stone, though rejected by mortals yet chosen and precious in God's sight, and like living stones, let yourselves be built into a spiritual house, to be a holy priesthood, to offer spiritual sacrifices acceptable to God through Jesus Christ. For it

stands in Scripture: 'See, I am laying in Zion a stone, a cornerstone chosen and precious; and whoever believes in him will not be put to shame.'" (*1 P* 2:4-6)

[St Paul writes] "I appeal to you therefore, brothers and sisters, by the mercies of God, to present your bodies as a living sacrifice, holy and acceptable to God, which is your spiritual worship. Do not be conformed to this world, but be transformed by the renewing of your minds, so that you may discern what is the will of God – what is good and acceptable and perfect." (*Rm* 12:1-2)

Catholic teaching

*Key passages from the Catechism
and other Church documents*

CCC 1323: "'At the Last Supper, on the night he was betrayed, our Saviour instituted the Eucharistic sacrifice of his Body and Blood. This he did in order to perpetuate the sacrifice of the cross throughout the ages until he should come again, and so to entrust to his beloved spouse, the Church, a memorial of his death and Resurrection: a sacrament of love, a sign of unity, a bond of charity, a Paschal banquet 'in which Christ is consumed, the mind is filled with grace, and a pledge of future glory is given to us." [*SC* 47]"

CCC 1364: "In the New Testament, the memorial takes on new meaning. When the Church celebrates the Eucharist, she commemorates Christ's Passover, and it is made

---

Illustration on facing page: *"Through the Mass, every generation of God's people is present to the one saving sacrifice of Christ, as it is re-presented on the altar"* (Image Code: T-01470-CW)

present: the sacrifice Christ offered once for all on the cross remains ever present. [Cf. *Heb* 7:25-27] 'As often as the sacrifice of the cross by which "Christ our Pasch has been sacrificed" is celebrated on the altar, the work of our redemption is carried out.' [*LG* 3; cf. *1 Co* 5:7]"

CCC 1366: "The Eucharist is thus a sacrifice because it re-presents (makes present) the sacrifice of the cross, because it is its memorial and because it applies its fruit."

CCC 1367: "The sacrifice of Christ and the sacrifice of the Eucharist are one single sacrifice."

CCC 1368: "The Eucharist is also the sacrifice of the Church. The Church which is the body of Christ participates in the offering of her head. With him, she herself is offered whole and entire. She unites herself to his intercession with the Father for all men… Christ's sacrifice present on the altar makes it possible for all generations of Christians to be united with his offering."

CCC 1371: "The Eucharistic sacrifice is also offered for the faithful departed who 'have died in Christ but are not yet wholly purified,' [Council of Trent (1562): *DS* 1743] so that they may be able to enter into the light and peace of Christ."

Wisdom from the saints

"Apart from the cross, there is no other ladder by which we may get to heaven." St Rose of Lima

Illustration on facing page: *"At Mass we unite ourselves with Christ and with each other in his offering to the Father. This perfect offering of praise and thanksgiving brings forgiveness and strength"* (Image Code: T-00856-OL)

"Trust all things to Jesus in the Blessed Sacrament and to Mary, Help of Christians, and you will see what miracles are." St John Bosco

"All the good works in the world are not equal to the Holy Sacrifice of the Mass because they are the works of men; but the Mass is the work of God. Martyrdom is nothing in comparison for it is but the sacrifice of man to God; but the Mass is the sacrifice of God for man." St John Vianney

"The Eucharist is a fire which inflames us." St John Damascene

Summary of core beliefs

- The Mass is a sacrifice because it re-presents the sacrifice of the cross for us and applies its power.

- Through the Sacrifice of the Mass, through the power of the Holy Spirit, we offer our lives to the Father with Christ, united with him in his death and Resurrection.

- The Mass is the most powerful prayer of thanksgiving and intercession; it brings great graces into the Church and into our lives; it brings forgiveness for our daily sins and purification for the faithful departed.

Practical suggestions

- Make a "morning offering" when you get up each day (there are different versions of this short prayer – you can look online).

- "Offer up" your daily sufferings and struggles to God and consciously unite them with the Sacrifice of the Mass.

- Bring a personal intention to each Mass so that you are consciously praying for a particular need. You can "offer your communion" for this intention.

- If you have a very special intention, or if someone has died, ask the priest (or arrange this through the parish office) to offer Mass for this intention.

- Hang a crucifix in your home to remind you of Christ's loving sacrifice.

- Try to follow the prayers of the Mass with more attention and devotion, entering into the words and intentions and making them your own, perhaps using a Sunday Missal or a Catholic App.

Prayer

Lord our God,
teach us to cherish in our hearts
the paschal mystery of your Son
by which you redeemed the world.
Watch over the gifts of grace your love has given us
and bring them to fulfilment in the glory of heaven.
We ask this through Christ our Lord.
R. Amen.

Sacred Banquet, Spiritual Food:
the Graces Given in Holy Communion

Reflection

There is a deep spiritual hunger within the heart of every
human being. We are like the Samaritan woman seeking
water at Jacob's well without understanding her deepest
thirst. St Augustine expressed this so clearly when he
wrote: "Almighty God, you have made us for yourself, and
our hearts are restless until they rest in you."

Jesus said, "I am the living bread that came down from
heaven. Whoever eats of this bread will live for ever; and
the bread that I will give for the life of the world is my
flesh." He fulfils this promise by giving us his Body and
Blood in the Eucharist as spiritual food and drink when
we receive Holy Communion. The Eucharist is a sacred
banquet which brings us into communion, not just with
Christ but, with the whole Church of heaven, purgatory
and earth.

The Catechism teaches that "the whole spiritual good
of the Church, namely Christ himself" is contained in the
blessed Eucharist. And St Thomas Aquinas writes that the
Eucharist is "the perfection of the spiritual life". These are
powerful phrases.

Illustration on facing page: *"A torrent of graces pours upon us from heaven through
the celebration of Mass and through the worthy reception of Holy Communion"*
(Image Code: T-00442-OL)

How often we look in the wrong places for happiness and meaning. Even in the spiritual life, we are often restless and dissatisfied, looking for the next novelty or fix. But in reality, everything we need for our lives as Christians – every gift, every blessing, every virtue – is given to us in Holy Communion. This is the Bread of Life, the whole spiritual good of the Church and of every Christian. Nothing is lacking. We just need to go deeper and understand the graces he is giving us, and be more open to them, so they can take effect in our lives.

We are encouraged to receive Holy Communion when we are at Mass, because the benefits are so great. We deepen our friendship and intimacy with Jesus Christ. The graces of baptism are renewed and increased. Our venial sins are forgiven. Our ability to love is strengthened. And we are given a foretaste of heaven itself. The Eucharist, as St Ignatius of Antioch wrote, "provides the medicine of immortality, the antidote for death, and the food that makes us live forever in Jesus Christ".

No one is truly worthy to meet Christ in this way. But all of us need to examine our conscience and prepare ourselves for so great an encounter. I need to live my life during the week in a way that is coherent with the Christian faith I profess each Sunday. I need to be continually open to conversion.

If there are any grave sins on my conscience then I need to go to Confession and receive absolution before coming to receive Holy Communion. This is to help me be honest with the Lord, and to know his mercy and forgiveness in

Confession, so I can meet him with an open heart and a pure conscience in Communion. He wants to welcome me in both sacraments, so that I can find true and lasting peace, instead of remaining unreconciled with him and with the Church. He calls me to Confession because he loves me and he wants to give me his peace.

Holy Scripture

For personal prayer, reflection and meditation

"The Samaritan woman said to Jesus, 'How is it that you, a Jew, ask a drink of me, a woman of Samaria?' (Jews do not share things in common with Samaritans.) Jesus answered her, 'If you knew the gift of God, and who it is that is saying to you, "Give me a drink", you would have asked him, and he would have given you living water.'" (*Jn* 4:9-10)

"Jesus said to them, 'I am the bread of life. Whoever comes to me will never be hungry, and whoever believes in me will never be thirsty... I am the living bread that came down from heaven. Whoever eats of this bread will live for ever; and the bread that I will give for the life of the world is my flesh... Those who eat my flesh and drink my blood have eternal life, and I will raise them up on the last day; for my flesh is true food and my blood is true drink. Those who eat my flesh and drink my blood abide in me, and I in them.'" (*Jn* 6:35, 51, 54-56)

[St Paul writes] "Whoever, therefore, eats the bread or drinks the cup of the Lord in an unworthy manner will be answerable

for the body and blood of the Lord. Examine yourselves, and only then eat of the bread and drink of the cup. For all who eat and drink without discerning the body, eat and drink judgement against themselves." (*1 Co* 11:27-29)

[Jesus says in the Book of Revelation] "Listen! I am standing at the door, knocking; if you hear my voice and open the door, I will come in to you and eat with you, and you with me." (*Rv* 3:20)

[St John writes in the Book of Revelation] "And the angel said to me, 'Write this: Blessed are those who are invited to the marriage supper of the Lamb.'" (*Rv* 19:9)

Catholic teaching

*Key passages from the Catechism
and other Church documents*

CCC 1415: "Anyone who desires to receive Christ in Eucharistic communion must be in the state of grace. Anyone aware of having sinned mortally must not receive Communion without having received absolution in the sacrament of penance."

CCC 1416: "Communion with the Body and Blood of Christ increases the communicant's union with the Lord, forgives his venial sins, and preserves him from grave sins. Since receiving this sacrament strengthens the bonds of charity between the communicant and Christ, it also reinforces the unity of the Church as the Mystical Body of Christ."

Illustration on facing page: *"Holy Communion unites us with Christ and with each other in his Body which is the Church. We are like jewels on his robe, lifted up to the Father through the power of the Holy Spirit"* (Image Code: T-00535-OL-V2)

CCC 1417: "The Church warmly recommends that the faithful receive Holy Communion when they participate in the celebration of the Eucharist; she obliges them to do so at least once a year."

CCC 1419: "Having passed from this world to the Father, Christ gives us in the Eucharist the pledge of glory with him. Participation in the Holy Sacrifice identifies us with his Heart, sustains our strength along the pilgrimage of this life, makes us long for eternal life, and unites us even now to the Church in heaven, the Blessed Virgin Mary, and all the saints."

CCC 1324: "'In the blessed Eucharist is contained the whole spiritual good of the Church, namely Christ himself, our Pasch.' [*PO* 5]"

CCC 1391: "The principal fruit of receiving the Eucharist in Holy Communion is an intimate union with Christ Jesus. Indeed, the Lord said: 'He who eats my flesh and drinks my blood abides in me, and I in him.' [*Jn* 6:56]"

Wisdom from the saints

"Not to go to Communion is like someone dying of thirst beside a spring." St John Vianney

"Our sharing in the Body and Blood of Christ has no other purpose than to transform us into that which we receive." Pope St Leo the Great

"Go often to Holy Communion. Go very often! This is your one remedy." St Thérèse of Lisieux

---

Illustration on facing page: *"Holy Communion brings us friendship and intimacy with our Saviour, Jesus Christ. We can rest in his loving embrace"* (Image Code: T-06226B-CW)

"All the good that is in me is due to Holy Communion. I owe everything to it. I feel this holy fire has transformed me completely." St Faustina

"When you have received him, stir up your heart to do him homage; speak to him about your spiritual life, gazing upon him in your soul where he is present for your happiness; welcome him as warmly as possible, and behave outwardly in such a way that your actions may give proof to all of his Presence." St Francis de Sales

"With all the strength of my soul I urge you young people to approach the Communion table as often as you can. Feed on this bread of angels whence you will draw all the energy you need to fight inner battles. Because true happiness, dear friends, does not consist in the pleasures of the world or in earthly things, but in peace of conscience, which we have only if we are pure in heart and mind." Blessed Pier Giorgio Frassati

Summary of core beliefs

- The Eucharist is the perfection of the spiritual life and Holy Communion brings us all the graces we need at this moment.

- Holy Communion brings forgiveness, intimacy with Christ, a growth in charity, deeper unity with all members of the Church, and a foretaste of heaven.

- We can prepare to receive Holy Communion worthily through prayer, repentance, and if necessary through making a good confession.

Practical suggestions

- Remember to keep the Eucharistic fast for one hour before Holy Communion – as a way of preparing for this great gift.

- Go to Confession, especially if you have any serious sins on your conscience, so that your heart can be open to receiving Christ in Holy Communion.

- Pray in thanksgiving for a few minutes after Mass, when others have left, and speak to the Lord about your needs and intentions.

- Try going to a weekday Mass, perhaps once a week, as an extra way of showing your love for the Lord and asking for his help.

- Bring a book of prayers to church that you can use before and after Mass in your personal devotion.

- Memorise some of the Eucharistic prayers and hymns from the Catholic tradition, e.g. Anima Christi, O Sacred Banquet, etc. (see "Prayers for Personal Devotion" at the end of this booklet for some ideas).

Prayer

Lord our God,
you have given us the true bread from heaven.
In the strength of this food
may we live always by your life
and rise in glory on the last day.
We ask this through Christ our Lord.
R. Amen.

Adoration of the Blessed Sacrament

Reflection

If you enter a Catholic church, you will nearly always spot a sanctuary lamp burning near the tabernacle, which is where the communion hosts are reserved after Mass. They are kept in this way for two reasons: first, so that Holy Communion can be taken to the sick and housebound when necessary; and second, so we can continue to worship Christ in the Holy Eucharist.

Jesus Christ remains present here in the communion hosts, in what we call the Blessed Sacrament. This is not just a metaphor or a symbol. He is truly present – Body, Blood, Soul and Divinity – in all his power and glory and majesty. So if a church appears to be empty, we know that we are never alone.

Whenever we come near to the tabernacle, even if the Blessed Sacrament is not exposed, we come into his hidden but powerful presence; heaven is laid open before us; and we can adore him and share our lives with him in a most intimate and profound way. We can speak to him, heart to heart. It is like Moses meeting the Lord in the burning bush, or the disciples walking up the mountain with Christ at the time of his Transfiguration.

Illustration on facing page: *"The Presence of Christ in the Blessed Sacrament is like a blazing fire. We worship his glory and majesty with repentance, gratitude, reverence and praise"* (Image Code: T-02670-OL)

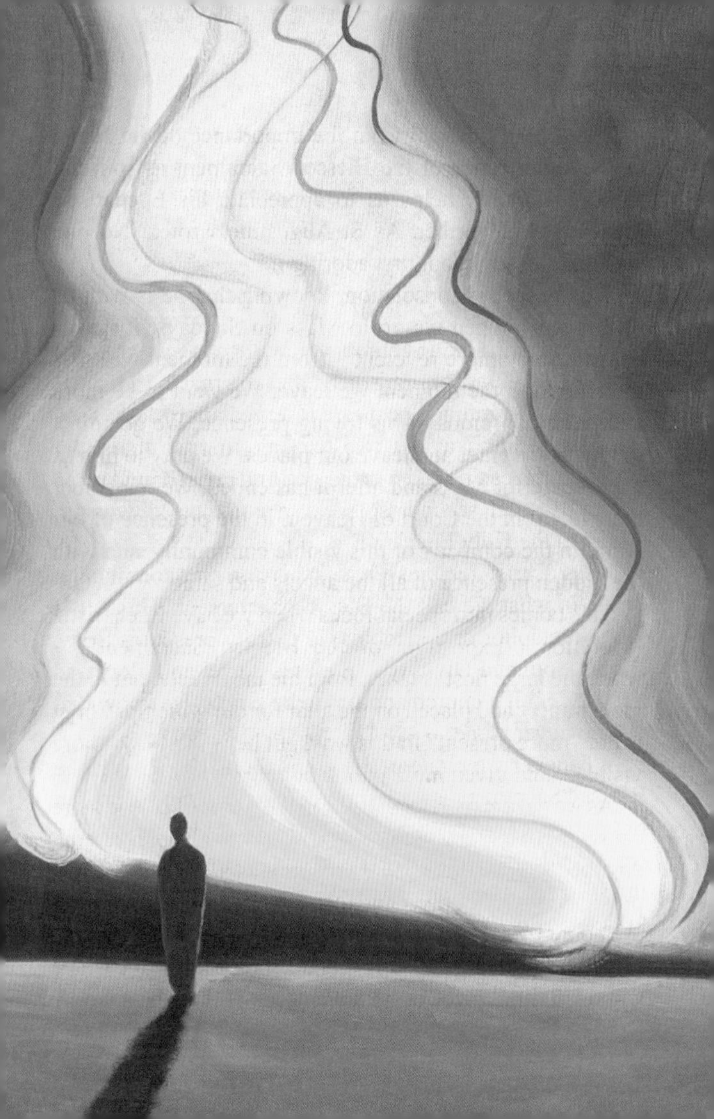

This doesn't detract from the importance of the Mass, or the significance of the Blessed Sacrament as spiritual food – it simply helps us to appreciate his Eucharistic presence even further. As St Augustine wrote: "No one eats that flesh without first adoring it."

This is such a consolation, knowing that he is with us in this way. When we go to Mass on Sundays, it makes us want to be more reverent – from the moment we enter the church to the moment we leave. We want to be more and more conscious of his loving presence. We genuflect to him as we enter and leave our places. We pray to him as we prepare for Mass and after it has ended. We remember that we are in the Court of Heaven, in the presence of our King, in the company of this visible community, and with the hidden presence of all the angels and saints.

This comes into special focus when we have Eucharistic Adoration ("Exposition of the Blessed Sacrament") – when the large host is taken from the tabernacle, put in the monstrance, and placed on the altar for our worship. Christ is not "more present" in this way, but he is in a way "more visible", and given more public honour.

As we gaze at his Sacred Body in the host we become more conscious of his holy Presence, more attentive, more grateful. And because we are worshipping him as a community, in a public liturgy, our prayer and worship has more significance. We adore Christ as a community, in the name of the Church, bringing the praise and sorrow and intercession of the whole Church to him, together with the needs of the whole world.

And we unite ourselves with Christ, through the Holy Spirit, in his praise and thanksgiving to the Father.

If the period of Adoration can conclude with Benediction, when the priest or deacon blesses the congregation with the Sacred Host, then this is a fitting climax to the liturgy.

There are many beautiful traditions surrounding our worship of the Holy Eucharist. Public processions with the Blessed Sacrament allow our Eucharistic faith to become a witness to others, which strengthens our own faith and gives them an opportunity to encounter Christ. Longer periods of Exposition such as the Forty Hours Devotion and Eucharistic retreats encourage a community to deepen their love for the Eucharist. And some parishes and oratories have Perpetual Adoration, with a rota of worshippers, so that the praise and thanksgiving becomes unceasing.

Holy Scripture

For personal prayer, reflection and meditation

"The angel of the Lord appeared to Moses in a flame of fire out of a bush; he looked, and the bush was blazing, yet it was not consumed… God called to him out of the bush, 'Moses, Moses!' And he said, 'Here I am.' Then he said, 'Come no closer! Remove the sandals from your feet, for the place on which you are standing is holy ground.'" (*Ex* 3:2, 4-5)

"Six days later, Jesus took with him Peter and James and his brother John and led them up a high mountain, by themselves. And he was transfigured before them, and his

face shone like the sun, and his clothes became dazzling white… Suddenly a bright cloud overshadowed them, and from the cloud a voice said, 'This is my Son, the Beloved; with him I am well pleased; listen to him!'" (*Mt* 17:1-2, 5)

[St John writes in the Book of Revelation] "And in the midst of the lampstands I saw one like the Son of Man, clothed with a long robe and with a golden sash across his chest. His head and his hair were white as white wool, white as snow; his eyes were like a flame of fire, his feet were like burnished bronze, refined as in a furnace, and his voice was like the sound of many waters. In his right hand he held seven stars, and from his mouth came a sharp, two-edged sword, and his face was like the sun shining with full force." (*Rv* 1:13-16)

[St John writes in the Book of Revelation] "Then I heard every creature in heaven and on earth and under the earth and in the sea, and all that is in them, singing, 'To the one seated on the throne and to the Lamb be blessing and honour and glory and might for ever and ever!' And the four living creatures said, 'Amen!' And the elders fell down and worshipped." (*Rv* 5:13-14)

Catholic teaching

*Key passages from the Catechism
and other Church documents*

CCC 1378: "*Worship of the Eucharist*. In the liturgy of the Mass we express our faith in the Real Presence of Christ under the species of bread and wine by, among other ways, genuflecting or bowing deeply as a sign of adoration of the Lord. 'The Catholic Church has always offered and still offers to the sacrament of the Eucharist the cult of adoration, not only during Mass, but also outside of it, reserving the consecrated hosts with the utmost care, exposing them to the solemn veneration of the faithful, and carrying them in procession.' [Paul VI, *MF* 56]"

CCC 1380: "In his Eucharistic presence, he remains mysteriously in our midst as the one who loved us and gave himself up for us, [cf. *Ga* 2:20] and he remains under signs that express and communicate this love: 'The Church and the world have a great need for Eucharistic worship. Jesus awaits us in this sacrament of love. Let us not refuse the time to go to meet him in adoration, in contemplation full of faith, and open to making amends for the serious offences and crimes of the world. Let our adoration never cease.' [John Paul II, *Dominicae Cenae*, 3]"

Sacramentum Caritatis 66: "The act of adoration outside Mass prolongs and intensifies all that takes place during the liturgical celebration itself. Indeed, 'only in adoration can a profound and genuine reception mature. And it is precisely this personal encounter with the Lord that then strengthens the social mission contained in the Eucharist, which seeks to break down not only the walls that separate the Lord and ourselves, but also and especially the walls that separate us from one another'. (Pope Benedict)"

Illustration on facing page: *"We follow Christ the Good Shepherd in procession. He leads us out of darkness, through the power of the Holy Spirit, to meet the Father face to face"* (Image Code: T-01685A-CW)

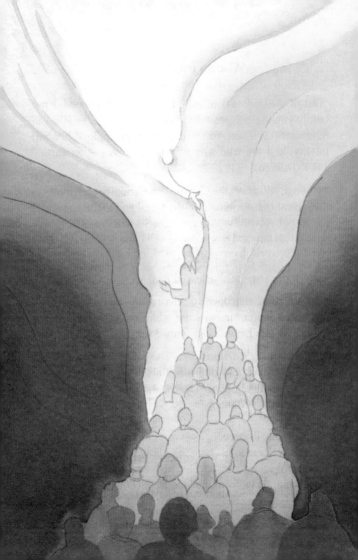

Wisdom from the saints
(And from Tolkien!)

"Out of the darkness of my life, so much frustrated, I put before you the one great thing to love on earth: the Blessed Sacrament ... There you will find romance, glory, honour, fidelity, and the true way of all your loves upon earth."
J R R Tolkien

"Through adoration, the Christian mysteriously contributes to the radical transformation of the world and to the sowing of the gospel. Anyone who prays to the Saviour draws the whole world with him and raises it to God." Pope St John Paul II

"Jesus in the Blessed Sacrament is the Living Heart of each of our parishes." Blessed Paul VI

"Do not think that Jesus Christ is forgetful of you, since he has left you, as the greatest memorial and pledge of his love, himself in the Most Holy Sacrament of the Altar."
St Alphonsus Liguori

"When the Sisters are exhausted, up to their eyes in work; when all seems to go awry, they spend an hour in prayer before the Blessed Sacrament. This practice has never failed to bear fruit: they experience peace and strength."
St Teresa of Calcutta

Summary of core beliefs

- Jesus Christ, true God and true man, is present in the consecrated hosts that are reserved outside Mass.

- We can worship his Eucharistic presence and draw close to him whenever we enter a Catholic church and pray before the tabernacle.

- Exposition of the Blessed Sacrament, Benediction, and Eucharistic processions are powerful ways of adoring Christ and expressing our faith in him.

Practical suggestions

- Get into the habit of making "a visit" to a Catholic church near home or work or college, and having a few minutes to pray and adore the Lord before the tabernacle.

- Find somewhere you can go to Exposition and Benediction, even if it means having to travel outside your parish.

- Make a mini-pilgrimage, perhaps with family or friends, to a Eucharistic shrine in your diocese, to a church where they have Perpetual Adoration, or to the Blessed Sacrament chapel in your Cathedral.

- Try to take part in a local Eucharistic procession on the Feast of Corpus Christi.

Prayer

Lord our God,
may we always give due honour
to the sacramental presence of the Lamb
who was slain for us.
May our faith be rewarded
by the vision of his glory,
who lives and reigns forever and ever.
R. Amen.

"Love One Another as I Have Loved You": The Implications of the Mass for Service and Mission

Reflection

The sacrament of the Eucharist is sometimes called "the Mass" (*Missa*) because it "concludes with the sending forth (*missio*) of the faithful, so that they may fulfil God's will in their daily lives." (*CCC* 1332) This mission is not just an optional appendix to the Eucharist, it is part of its inner meaning.

This is underlined in the Gospel of St John. At the Last Supper, where we might expect to learn about the Institution of the Eucharist ("This is my body…"), instead we see Jesus kneeling before his disciples and washing their feet. There is no contradiction between St John and the other Gospels, in fact there is a great unity. We understand that the self-giving love of the Eucharist, which looks forward to the sacrifice of the cross, is inseparable from a self-giving love for one's neighbour. As Jesus says: "If I, your Lord and Teacher, have washed your feet, you also ought to wash one another's feet… I give you a new commandment, that you love one another. Just as I have loved you, you also should love one another."

Illustration on facing page: *"The people we carry in our hearts can be touched and transformed by our prayer, our love, and our service"* (Image Code: T-00532-OL)

In the Eucharist, we come to understand Christ's immense love for us. He loves us even when we do not deserve that love. He gives his life for us on the cross. He gives himself to us sacramentally in his Body and Blood. Our response – personal and communal – is to do the same for others: to love family, friends, colleagues, neighbours; to love all those we meet, and especially the most needy.

The Eucharist transforms who we are and transforms the way we love. In Christ, we no longer live for ourselves, but for him, and for others. His teaching ("love your enemies… bless those who curse you…give without any hope of return…take up your cross…") which might have seemed very abstract, becomes full of meaning, because we want to love him and our neighbour in return for his love.

This self-giving is built into the structure of the Eucharist. The collection is meant to be for the needs of the poor and not just for the church. And by receiving Holy Communion, I become one with all the members of Christ's body, including the poor and the marginalised. As St John Chrysostom wrote: "You have tasted the Blood of the Lord, yet you do not recognise your brother… God freed you from all your sins and invited you here, but you have not become more merciful."

Pope Benedict wrote:

Union with Christ is also union with all those to whom he gives himself. I cannot possess Christ just for myself; I can belong to him only in union with all those who have become, or who will become, his own. Communion draws me out of myself towards him, and thus also towards unity with all Christians. We become "one body", completely joined in a single existence. Love of God and love of neighbour are now truly united: God incarnate draws us all to himself.

(Deus Caritas Est)

The Eucharist is a school of charity, justice and peace. It is also, as Pope Benedict wrote, a school of mission.

The love that we celebrate in the sacrament is not something we can keep to ourselves. By its very nature it demands to be shared with all. What the world needs is God's love; it needs to encounter Christ and to believe in him. The Eucharist is thus the source and summit not only of the Church's life, but also of her mission: 'an authentically Eucharistic Church is a missionary Church.'

(Sacramentum Caritatis 84)

Holy Scripture

For personal prayer, reflection and meditation

"Jesus, knowing that the Father had given all things into his hands, and that he had come from God and was going to God, got up from the table, took off his outer robe, and tied a towel around himself. Then he poured water into a basin and began to wash the disciples' feet and to wipe them with the towel that was tied around him." *(Jn 13:3-5)*

[Jesus said] "'This is my commandment, that you love one another as I have loved you. No one has greater love than this, to lay down one's life for one's friends. You are my friends if you do what I command you.'" (*Jn* 15:12-14)

[Jesus said] "'But I say to you that listen, Love your enemies, do good to those who hate you, bless those who curse you, pray for those who abuse you. If anyone strikes you on the cheek, offer the other also; and from anyone who takes away your coat do not withhold even your shirt. Give to everyone who begs from you; and if anyone takes away your goods, do not ask for them again. Do to others as you would have them do to you.'" (*Lk* 6:27-31)

[Jesus said] "'For I was hungry and you gave me food, I was thirsty and you gave me something to drink, I was a stranger and you welcomed me, I was naked and you gave me clothing, I was sick and you took care of me, I was in prison and you visited me... Truly I tell you, just as you did it to one of the least of these who are members of my family, you did it to me.'" (*Mt* 25:35-36, 40)

Catholic teaching

*Key passages from the Catechism
and other Church documents*

CCC 1351: "From the very beginning Christians have brought, along with the bread and wine for the Eucharist, gifts to share with those in need. This custom of the

---

Illustration on facing page: *"After Mass, if we stay close to Christ, his love can help us love those around us in practical ways, especially the poor, the weak and the most needy"* (Image Code: T-00651-OL)

collection, ever appropriate, is inspired by the example of Christ who became poor to make us rich. [Cf. *1 Co* 16:1; *2 Co* 8:9]"

CCC 1397: "The Eucharist commits us to the poor. To receive in truth the Body and Blood of Christ given up for us, we must recognise Christ in the poorest, his brethren."

"This sacramental 'mysticism' is social in character, for in sacramental communion I become one with the Lord, like all the other communicants. As St Paul says, 'Because there is one bread, we who are many are one body, for we all partake of the one bread.' (*1 Co* 10:17) Union with Christ is also union with all those to whom he gives himself. I cannot possess Christ just for myself... Love of God and love of neighbour are now truly united: God incarnate draws us all to himself." (*Deus Caritas Est* 14, Pope Benedict)

"Lived in this way, not only the Sunday Eucharist but the whole of Sunday becomes a great school of charity, justice and peace. The presence of the Risen Lord in the midst of his people becomes an undertaking of solidarity, a compelling force for inner renewal, an inspiration to change the structures of sin in which individuals, communities and at times entire peoples are entangled." (*Dies Domini* 73, Pope John Paul II)

"We cannot approach the Eucharistic table without being drawn into the mission which, beginning in the very heart

Illustration on facing page: *"At Mass, we share in the life, death and resurrection of Christ. As missionary disciples, our vocation is to share this amazing news with others"* (Image Code: T-01330-OL)

of God, is meant to reach all people. Missionary outreach is thus an essential part of the Eucharistic form of the Christian life." (*Sacramentum Caritatis* 84, Pope Benedict)

Wisdom from the saints

"Where will you get the joy of loving? In the Eucharist, in Holy Communion. Jesus has made Himself the Bread of Life to give us life. Night and day, he is there. If you really want to grow in love, come back to the Eucharist, come back to that adoration." St Teresa of Calcutta

"In each of our lives Jesus comes as the Bread of Life – to be eaten, to be consumed by us. This is how he loves us. Then Jesus comes in our human life as the hungry one, the other, hoping to be fed with the Bread of our life, our hearts by loving, and our hands by serving." St Teresa of Calcutta

"The Eucharist involves more than just receiving; it also involves satisfying the hunger of Christ. He says, 'Come to Me.' He is hungry for souls." St Teresa of Calcutta

"We cannot do everything, and there is a sense of liberation in realising that. This enables us to do something, and to do it very well. It may be incomplete, but it is a beginning, a step along the way, an opportunity for the Lord's grace to enter and do the rest." Blessed Oscar Romero

Summary of core beliefs

- The experience of Christ's sacrificial love in the Eucharist motivates us to love others as he has loved us.

- The Eucharist strengthens us to love our neighbour, to recognise each person as our brother or sister, and to be open to the needs of all – especially the poor and forgotten.

- The beauty of Christ's love in the Eucharist is such an amazing gift and brings such joy that we long to share this good news with others as missionary disciples.

Practical suggestions

- Make a new effort to greet people after Mass (e.g. outside the church) and spend a few minutes getting to know them.

- If there is tea and coffee after your Mass, try to overcome your shyness or busyness and go to it. If there is not, you could offer to your priest to organise this yourself!

- Think about how your everyday relationships (with family, friends, colleagues) reflect the love of Christ, and how your love could be purer and more generous.

- If you have time, consider volunteering for a local project e.g. within your parish, or your community, or the SVP, or through one of the diocesan Caritas networks.

- Always be on the lookout for those who are marginalised in any way.

- Be more confident in living and sharing your Catholic faith; take more risks in speaking about your Catholic faith with others; pray for opportunities to share your faith or invite people to Catholic events.

- Consider joining or starting in your parish a group committed to social outreach or mission, like the St Vincent de Paul Society (for the Corporal Works of Mercy) or the Legion of Mary (for the Spiritual Works of Mercy).

Prayer

Lord,
give to our hearts
the light of faith and the fire of love,
that we may worship in spirit and in truth
our God and Lord, present in this sacrament,
who lives and reigns forever and ever.
R. Amen.

Prayers for Personal Devotion

For use in church as you pray before the Blessed Sacrament, or after receiving Holy Communion

Prayer of St Francis of Assisi

We adore you, most holy Lord Jesus Christ, here, and in all your churches throughout all the world; and we bless you, because, by your holy cross, you have redeemed the world.

Shorter form from the Stations of the Cross:

We adore you, O Christ, and we praise you, because by your holy cross you have redeemed the world.

Anima Christi

Soul of Christ, sanctify me. Body of Christ, save me. Blood of Christ, inebriate me. Water from the side of Christ, wash me.

Passion of Christ, strengthen me. O good Jesus, hear me. Within Thy wounds hide me. Suffer me not to be separated from Thee.

From the malicious enemy defend me. In the hour of my death call me. And bid me come unto Thee. That with Thy saints I may praise Thee. Forever and ever, Amen.

O Sacrum Convivium

O sacred banquet, in which Christ is received, the memory of his Passion is renewed, the mind is filled with grace, and a pledge of future glory is given to us.

V. Thou didst give them bread from heaven:

R. Containing in itself all sweetness.

O God, who under a wonderful Sacrament hast left us a memorial of Thy Passion; grant us, we beseech Thee, so to reverence the sacred mysteries of Thy Body and Blood, that we may ever feel within ourselves the fruit of Thy Redemption: Who livest and reignest for ever and ever. Amen.

Lamb of God

Lamb of God, you take away the sins of the world, have mercy on us.

Lamb of God, you take away the sins of the world, have mercy on us.

Lamb of God, you take away the sins of the world, grant us peace.

Divine Mercy prayer

Eternal Father, I offer you the body and blood, soul and divinity, of your dearly beloved son, Our Lord Jesus Christ, in atonement for our sins and those of the whole world.

Prayer to the Sacred Heart

Sacred Heart of Jesus, I put my trust in Thee. Sacred Heart of Jesus, have mercy on me.

Consecration to Jesus through Mary
by St Louis de Montfort

I am all yours and all I have is yours, O dear Jesus, through Mary, your holy Mother.

Prayer of the priest before he receives
Holy Communion at Mass

Lord Jesus Christ, Son of the living God, who, by the will of the Father and the work of the Holy Spirit, through your Death gave life to the world, free me by this, your most holy Body and Blood, from all my sins and from every evil; keep me always faithful to your commandments, and never let me be parted from you.

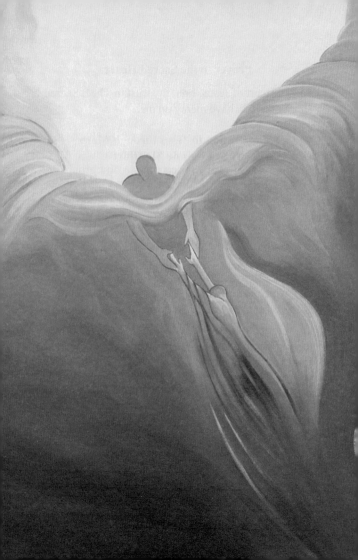

How to Run a Faith Sharing Group Using this Booklet

You might want to use the chapters of this booklet as a basis for some group discussion with friends, or your parish might want to organise faith sharing groups for a few weeks using these materials. It could be a six week programme. It is best if each member of the group has their own personal copy of the booklet.

General tips

The ideal size for a faith sharing group is from six to ten people, but you may wish to form groups of eight to twelve people, which means you still have a reasonable number if one or two cannot attend a given meeting. It is sometimes better to split a larger group in two for the discussion part, e.g. to meet as a large group, but to have two groups of six when you discuss, rather than one of twelve.

Be clear about when and where you are meeting. Create a welcoming environment in the room where you meet. It can be helpful to have a central focus in the room such as an open Bible, a crucifix and a candle. Have tea and coffee available as people arrive (and perhaps biscuits and cake). Make sure the host welcomes people and introduces them to each other. Stick to time and finish when you say you will finish (e.g. after one hour).

Illustration on facing page: *"If we stay close to Christ in faith, hope and love, he will lift us out of darkness and give us a share in his light, joy and peace"* (Image Code: T-01406-OL)

Each session might have a balance of prayer, sharing, discussion, Scripture, reflection, silence, and thinking about how to put these ideas into practice. It's fine to shorten things and adapt these materials if that will suit your group. Prayer can take different forms: you can choose whatever way will work for your group. Silence is an important part of the process, so don't be afraid to pause during your prayer time or, indeed, during the reflection time, for some quiet.

You can listen to the reflection and meditate on the Scripture readings that are given in each chapter. As you reflect and discuss together, ensure each person who wants to talk is given an opportunity to share. This is a chance to reflect on your experience and share your lives in a trusting environment. But no one needs to talk unless they want to, and no one person should dominate the conversation.

The role of the group leader

A group leader is not necessarily a catechist or someone who takes on a teaching role, but a fellow participant with particular responsibility for facilitating the group. They are responsible for: getting things ready beforehand in the meeting room; welcoming and introducing people to each other; encouraging the group to speak and listen and share their faith with each other; facilitating the reflection and discussion; ensuring that each participant has the opportunity to speak if they wish; timekeeping; ensuring that everything in the group takes place according to parish and diocesan safeguarding expectations (if necessary by liaising with the parish safeguarding representative).

A possible structure for a group session

Timings are just rough suggestions

Introduction [15 mins]

Gathering: tea and coffee are available, and perhaps some biscuits and cakes, as people arrive. Welcome and introductions, followed by an opening prayer (e.g. begin with a moment of quiet and then pray the Our Father and the Hail Mary). You may wish to have some informal introductory discussion, e.g. "How are you? How was your week? What things are on your mind? Have you had any thoughts about last week's session?"

Holy Scripture [5 mins]

The leader asks someone to read out loud the Scripture passages printed in this week's chapter, followed by a brief pause for silent reflection.

Reflection [10 mins]

The leader asks someone to read out the Reflection at the beginning of the chapter, or for people to read it quietly themselves. Followed by a longer pause: for silent reflection on the Reflection and on the accompanying images.

Main Discussion and Faith Sharing [20 mins]

You can use these general questions as a basis for your discussion in each session:

(i) What thoughts and personal responses do you have about the Scripture readings, about the Reflection, and about the paintings reproduced here?

(ii) How do these ideas fit with your own experience of faith and of life in the Church?

(iii) What implications do these ideas have for your own life and faith, and for the life of your parish community?

Putting it into Practice [15 mins]

Read the Practical Suggestions in the chapter and then reflect on these two questions together:

(i) What do you think of these practical suggestions? Which of them might work best for you?

(ii) What other things could you do, individually or as a community, to make the themes in this chapter more central to your lives?

Concluding Remarks [5 mins]

Encourage people to come to the next meeting, and to reflect on the written materials for this session and for the coming session during the week. Finish with a final prayer (e.g. pray together the prayer printed in the relevant chapter and conclude with the Glory Be).